MW01489758

2024 iMac M4 User Guide

Troubleshooting, Setup Instructions and How to use iMac with M4 Chip, Manual for Beginners and Seniors

By

Tatiana Dash

Disclaimer:

CONTENTS

INTRODUCTION

The **2024 iMac with the M4 chip** is a true testament to Apple's commitment to blending beauty and performance, and as a long-time fan, I couldn't be more thrilled. Apple has outdone itself with this model, introducing a sleek, vibrant display, enhanced processing power, and impressive multitasking capabilities that make it a joy to use. The iMac's all-in-one design is still as stunning as ever- ultra-thin, minimalist, and crafted with such elegance that it feels more like an art piece than a computer.

The M4 chip itself is nothing short of a game-changer. It's fast, responsive, and incredibly efficient, making everything from simple web browsing to complex creative tasks feel effortless. Apps launch in a snap, multitasking is smooth and fluid, and power-intensive applications like video editing software run seamlessly, all without the slightest hiccup. The integration of the chip with macOS takes efficiency to another level, optimizing performance while keeping power consumption low.

One of my favourite improvements is in the display. The colours are vibrant, and the detail is so sharp that photos, videos, and even text appear crisp and lifelike. Working on this screen feels immersive, and it's perfect for everything from design work to binge-watching a favourite series.

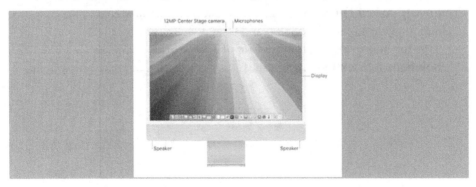

The 2024 iMac also has a fantastic suite of connectivity options. The upgraded USB-C and Thunderbolt ports allow for easy connections with all my peripherals, and I appreciate the seamless compatibility with other Apple devices- AirPods pair instantly, file sharing via AirDrop is lightning-fast, and Handoff makes working across devices feel like magic.

In short, the 2024 iMac with the M4 chip feels like a love letter to long-time Apple enthusiasts, delivering on the design, performance, and functionality that make the iMac an iconic choice. If you're looking for a machine that's both powerful and elegantly designed, this model will remind you why you fell in love with the iMac in the first place.

Apple's new iMac with M4

With the M4 chip, you will expect it to deliver up to 1.7x faster performance for productivity and 2.1x faster graphics performance for tasks like photo editing and gaming compared to the M1 iMac. It's also available in fresh colours and includes a nano-texture display option, a 12MP Center Stage camera, Thunderbolt 4 connectivity, and up to 32GB of unified memory.

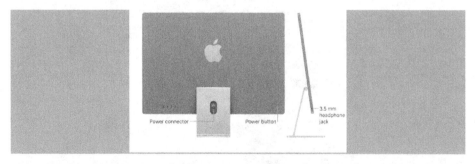

Enhanced by Apple Intelligence on macOS Sequoia 15.1, it brings systemwide tools for text refinement, an upgraded Siri, and privacy-focused AI features, with expanded capabilities like ChatGPT integration and custom emoji rolling out, in December 2024.

This exciting device now includes all powerful Writing Tools that will enable text rewriting, proofreading, and summarization in both Apple and third-party apps. The era of Apple Intelligence ensures privacy with on-device processing and Private Cloud Compute, allowing free access to ChatGPT with privacy safeguards.

The redesigned Siri, accessible from anywhere on the desktop, now supports typed requests for quiet spaces. Available in seven vibrant colours, the iMac also features a 24-inch 4.5K Retina display with an optional nano-texture glass for reduced glare, without compromising image quality, making it ideal for well-lit spaces.

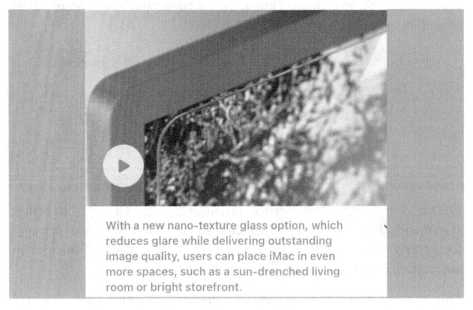

With a new nano-texture glass option, which reduces glare while delivering outstanding image quality, users can place iMac in even more spaces, such as a sun-drenched living room or bright storefront.

Colour-matched accessories with USB-C ports add convenience, enabling single-cable charging for all devices.

The built-in 12-megapixel camera supports 1080p HD video and Desk View, ideal for video calls and content creation. Combined with studio-quality microphones and a six-speaker system with Dolby Atmos support, the M4 iMac is designed for a top-tier audio and video experience.

This means that video calls are upgraded with the 12MP Center Stage camera, which will keep you centred, while the Desk View will allow a wide-angle top-down view for showing a workspace or project, and the sound experience is enhanced with a studio-quality three-microphone array with the immersive six-speaker system.

With advanced connectivity, the iMac M4 supports four USB-C ports with Thunderbolt 4, which will enable superfast data transfers and connection to up to two 6K displays. You will benefit from Wi-Fi 6E, Bluetooth 5.3, and secure Touch ID with Fast User Switching.

The macOS Sequoia enhances the iMac experience with iPhone Mirroring, the Highlights feature in Safari, Distraction Control, and Personalized Spatial Audio for gaming. The new Passwords app stores credentials, and you can customize video calls with new backgrounds. Not forgetting Eco-friendly- the iMac incorporates 100% recycled aluminium, gold, tin, and copper in its build and uses entirely fibre-based packaging.

I particularly love its support for high-speed peripherals and up to two external displays in higher-end configurations. Plus, the reintroduction of the SD card reader, a feature creatives appreciated in previous MacBook Pro models.

First Impression

When the iMac M4 chip is delivered to you, you will likely get the essentials for immediate setup and use. Here's what you'll find in the box:

1. **iMac Unit**: The sleek 24-inch iMac features a powerful M4 chip with an ultra-thin design, vibrant colours (like green, yellow,

purple, etc.), and a 4.5K Retina display for a clear and immersive visual experience.

2. **Magic Keyboard**: This now includes an upgraded Touch ID for quick and secure logins, with Fast User Switching support, making it easy to toggle between user profiles.

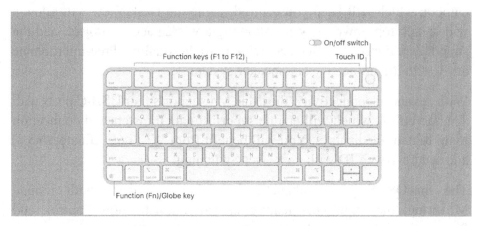

3. **Magic Mouse or Magic Trackpad**: Apple includes a Magic Mouse by default, and you may have the option to upgrade to the Magic Trackpad, depending on your choice or customizations during purchase.

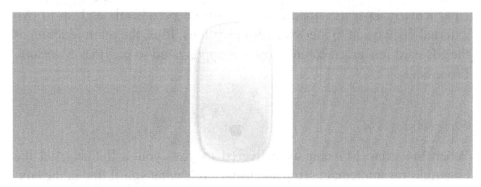

4. **Power Cable and Power Adapter**: A colour-matched, fabric-wrapped power cable with an external power adapter that connects magnetically to the iMac.

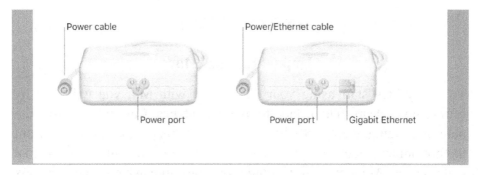

Power cable   Power/Ethernet cable

Power port   Power port   Gigabit Ethernet

5. **USB-C to Lightning Cable**: Used to charge your Magic Keyboard and Magic Mouse/Trackpad.

6. **Quick Start Guide and Apple Stickers**: Includes a basic setup guide to get you started and Apple logo stickers, typically matching the iMac's colour for a cohesive aesthetic.

The setup is designed to be straightforward, with easy-to-connect accessories that integrate well with the iMac's functionality and the upgraded M4 performance.

INITIAL SETUP

Unpacking the iMac

To safely kick start using your 2024 iMac with M4, you will start by setting up a clean, flat surface to avoid scratches. Carefully remove the outer packaging, then gently lift the iMac from its box, supporting it from the bottom and sides to protect the screen and prevent damage to internal components. Apple typically includes pull-tabs to make removing the box contents easier.

1. **Remove Plastic and Foam**: Carefully peel off protective plastic layers and foam padding around the iMac and accessories.

2. **Positioning**: Place the iMac on a sturdy desk, ideally near a power outlet. It's important to choose a location that supports good ventilation and minimizes glare, especially if you've chosen the nano-texture glass option, which reduces reflections.

3. **Screen Protection**: Avoid direct sunlight on the display, and, if possible, use a screen protector to keep the 4.5K Retina display scratch-free.

Check that your colour-matched keyboard is intact and test the Touch ID functionality.

Ensure the included mouse (or optional Magic Trackpad) is functioning and undamaged.

The power cable should connect magnetically to the iMac and come with a colour-matched, fabric-wrapped cord for easy identification. Confirm that the power adapter is also included and matches the colour.

Use this to charge your Magic Keyboard and Magic Mouse/Trackpad.

Once all components are accounted for and positioned, you're ready to proceed with the power-on and initial setup steps.

Connect your iMac

1. Setting Up the Power Cable

- Start by attaching the **magnetic power connector** to the iMac's back panel. This connector is designed for easy, secure attachment and detachment.

- Plug the other end into the **power adapter**, then connect the adapter to a power outlet.

- Make sure the power adapter and outlet are close to the iMac to keep the area organized.

2. Connecting the Magic Keyboard and Magic Mouse (or Trackpad)

- **Magic Keyboard**: Turn on the Magic Keyboard by sliding the power switch on its side, typically identified by a green indicator.

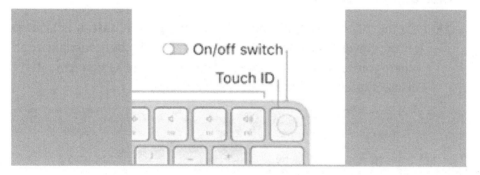

- **Magic Mouse**: Similarly, switch on the Magic Mouse from its underside.

- Use the **USB-C to Lightning cable** included in the box to connect both the keyboard and mouse to the iMac for initial pairing. Afterwards, they should connect automatically via Bluetooth when within range.

3. Overview of Available Ports and Connections

- The iMac includes **four USB-C ports**, all of which support Thunderbolt 4 for fast data transfer, charging, and connectivity with external displays or storage devices.

- **Audio Jack**: A standard 3.5mm headphone jack is on the left side, suitable for wired headphones and speakers.

- **Network Options**: The Wi-Fi 6E and Bluetooth 5.3 along with an **Ethernet port** (optional on some models) integrated into the power adapter.

With all cables and peripherals in place, your iMac is now ready to power on and guide you through the setup process.

Powering on for the First Time

Power Button Location

- On the 2024 iMac with the M4 chip, the **power button** is located on the lower backside of the iMac, toward the bottom-right edge when you're facing the screen. This placement is convenient yet discreet, preserving the iMac's sleek design.

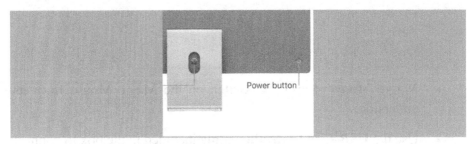

Power button

- To power on, press and hold the button for a second until you see the Apple logo on the display. The iMac will start up and guide you through the initial setup process on-screen.

Adjusting the iMac's Screen Angle and Positioning

- **Screen Angle**: The iMac's display is mounted on a stand with a slight tilt mechanism, allowing you to adjust the angle for an optimal view. Hold the edges of the display gently, then tilt it up or down until it feels comfortable for your viewing height and seating position.

Ensure you place the iMac on a stable surface with enough space to allow airflow from the rear vents. Ideally, position the iMac at eye level to minimize neck strain and ensure a comfortable viewing experience. If possible, avoid direct sunlight on the screen to reduce glare, especially if you opted for the standard glass option over the nano-texture glass.

SOFTWARE SETUP

Setting Up macOS for the First Time

After powering on your iMac, you'll be guided through the macOS setup process. This includes several steps to customize your device settings and get connected.

1. Language and Region Selection

The first screen will prompt you to choose your **preferred language**. Scroll through the list and select the one you're most comfortable with; this language will be used across the entire macOS interface.

Next, choose your **region** or **country** to ensure accurate time zone settings and access to region-specific features like dictation languages, currency formats, and date/time display.

2. Connecting to Wi-Fi

The setup assistant will prompt you to select a **Wi-Fi network**. Pick your network from the list of available options and enter the Wi-Fi password when prompted. If your iMac is connected via Ethernet, this step will be skipped, as the wired connection will be automatically detected.

A stable internet connection is essential for signing in with your Apple ID, syncing iCloud, and downloading software updates. Make sure your Wi-

Fi connection is secure, especially if you're using the iMac in a public or shared space.

Once connected, the iMac will move on to Apple ID setup, data migration options, and configuring your account preferences to tailor the experience to your needs.

Signing in with Your Apple ID

1. **Apple ID Prompt**: After connecting to Wi-Fi, you'll be asked to sign in with your Apple ID.

This account links your iMac to Apple services like iCloud, the App Store, and Find My. Type in your Apple ID email and password to log in.

If you need to move your data from your old device to your new iMac, you will follow data migration option, after signing into your Apple account

But, if you don't have an Apple ID, select the option to create a new one, and follow the on-screen instructions.

Create apple ID

To create an Apple ID, you can follow these steps:

1. Select "Create Your Apple ID." Or Go to the official Apple ID website if you want to use another device to create your ID, and click 'Create Your Apple ID'.

2. **Enter Personal Information**: Fill in your details, including your first and last name, country, birth date, and email address. This email will serve as your Apple ID.

3. **Choose a Password**: Create a strong password that meets Apple's requirements. You'll need to re-enter it to confirm.

4. **Set Up Security Questions**: Apple will ask you to select and answer three security questions. These questions will help you recover your account if you forget your password.

5. **Agree to Terms and Conditions**: Read and agree to Apple's terms and conditions.

6. **Verify Email**: Check your email inbox for a verification email from Apple. Click the link in the email to confirm your account.

7. **Enable Two-Factor Authentication (Optional)**: Apple recommends setting up two-factor authentication for added security.

After these steps, your Apple ID will be ready to use for services like iCloud, the App Store, and Apple Music. Note that you can always create an Apple ID directly on your iMac, iPhone, or other Apple devices by going to **Settings > Sign in to your iPhone/Mac > Create Apple ID**.

If you have two-factor authentication enabled, you'll receive a code on another trusted Apple device. Enter this code on your iMac to verify your identity.

Once signed in, your iMac will sync with iCloud, making your photos, documents, and settings available across all your Apple devices.

Setting Up Touch ID

The Touch ID setup is part of the initial macOS setup, allowing you to secure your iMac and use fingerprint authentication for tasks like unlocking your Mac and making purchases.

Locate Touch ID Setup: In the setup assistant, you'll see a prompt to set up Touch ID.

Place Finger on Touch ID: The Touch ID sensor is built into your Magic Keyboard. Place your finger on the sensor without pressing down. Lift and rest your finger repeatedly to let the sensor capture different angles of your fingerprint.

Complete Setup: After several scans, you'll be prompted to adjust your grip and place the edges of your finger on the sensor. Once complete, macOS will save the fingerprint for quick access and authentication.

After setting up, you can add additional fingerprints in **System Settings** > **Touch ID & Password** for other fingers or users on the iMac.

Configuring Basic Settings

Display: Go to **System Preferences** > **Displays**. Adjust your display's brightness, resolution, and colour profile as needed. On compatible models, you can enable **True Tone** to adapt the display colour based on ambient light.

1. **Sound**: Head to **System Preferences** > **Sound**. Here, you can control the volume, adjust input/output settings, and select audio sources. To change system alert sounds, navigate to the "Sound Effects" tab.

2. **Dock and Menu Bar**: Customize your Dock by selecting **System Preferences** > **Dock & Menu Bar**. Here, you can adjust the Dock's size, position, and behaviour, such as auto-hide or magnification.

Setting up User Accounts

1. **Navigate to Users & Groups**: Open **System Preferences** > **Users & Groups**.

2. **Create a New Account**: Click the + icon to add a new user. Select the account type (Standard, Admin, and Managed with Parental Controls), and enter the full name, account name, password, and a password hint.

3. **Manage User Permissions**: If you're creating a Standard account, it will have limited access to system settings and applications. Admin accounts have full control, while "Managed" accounts can have parental controls and time limits.

Privacy and Security Settings

1. **Go to Security & Privacy**: In **System Preferences**, select **Security & Privacy**. Here, you can adjust key privacy settings, including location services, app permissions, and firewall settings.

2. **FileVault**: Enable **FileVault** for disk encryption to protect your data. This option can be found under the **FileVault** tab.

3. **Firewall**: Enable the **Firewall** to protect your iMac from unauthorized network connections.

4. **App Permissions**: Under the **Privacy** tab, you'll find various categories (Camera, Microphone, Location Services) where you can manage app permissions.

After configuring these essential settings, your iMac is already optimized for usability and security, tailored to your needs and privacy preferences.

Updating to the Latest macOS

Keeping your iMac's macOS up to date ensures you have the latest features, security patches, and bug fixes. Here's how to check for updates and enable automatic updates:

1. **Open System Settings**: Click the Apple menu (□) in the top-left corner of the screen and select **System Settings**. It used to be **System Preferences** on older versions of macOS.

2. **Select General > Software Update**: In System Settings, go to **General** and then select **Software Update**. Your iMac will automatically check for any available macOS updates.

3. **Check for Available Updates**: If an update is available, it will be displayed here with the option to download and install it.

Installing Updates

1. **Download the Update**: Click **Update Now** to start downloading the latest macOS version. This process may take some time, depending on your internet speed and the update's size.

2. **Install the Update**: Once the download is complete, a prompt will appear to install the update. Follow the on-screen instructions to proceed, and your iMac will restart to apply the updates.

3. **Finishing the Update**: After restarting, your iMac may display a progress bar. Let the installation finish, which may take a few minutes. Once completed, your iMac will reboot with the updated macOS version.

Enabling Automatic Updates

1. **Automatic Updates Option**: In the **Software Update** section, check the box for **Automatic Updates**. This option allows your iMac to automatically check, download, and install updates in the background.

2. **Customize Automatic Update Settings**: You can choose to install only certain updates (e.g., only security updates or system data files) by clicking **Advanced** in the Software Update settings. Select the options that suit your preferences for greater control.

Enabling automatic updates is recommended for improved security and access to the latest macOS features.

GET FAMILIAR WITH THE MACOS INTERFACE

Desktop Overview

The macOS desktop is the primary workspace where you interact with your applications and files. It features a clean and intuitive layout, with the background image customizable to suit your style. You'll find the **Trash** icon in the lower right corner, which is used for deleting files.

Exploring the Dock and Desktop Icons

Dock: The Dock is a prominent feature of macOS, located at the bottom (or side) of the screen.

It holds icons for your most-used applications, allowing quick access. You can customize it by dragging apps in or out, rearranging them, and even adding folders.

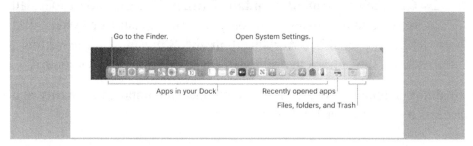

Desktop Icons: On the desktop, you can place files, folders, and application shortcuts for easy access. The default desktop icons include **Applications**, **Documents**, and **Downloads**, which help you organize your content efficiently.

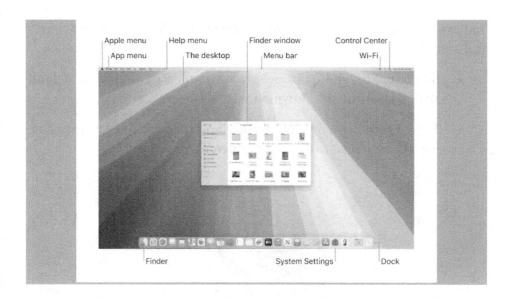

The Menu Bar

The **menu bar** runs along the top of the screen and provides access to various system functions and application menus. Key components include:

- **Apple Menu (☐)**: Access system settings, recent documents, and shutdown options.

- **Application Menu**: This changes depending on the active app and provides options like File, Edit, View, and Help.

- **Status Menus**: On the right side of the menu bar, you'll find status icons for Wi-Fi, battery life, and system notifications. Clicking these gives quick access to relevant settings.

Understanding Finder and File Organization

Finder is a file management application on macOS that allows you to navigate through your files and folders. It's essential for file organization and can be accessed by clicking the Finder icon in the Dock. Key features include:

- **Sidebar**: Provides quick access to common locations like **iCloud Drive**, **Documents**, **Downloads**, and external drives.

- **View Options**: You can change how files are displayed (icons, lists, or columns) to suit your preferences.

- **Tagging**: Use tags to categorize files and folders, making it easier to locate them later. Right-click on any file to add a tag.

By familiarizing yourself with these aspects of the macOS interface, you'll enhance your productivity and overall user experience.

System Settings and Control Center

Accessing System Preferences

Always access System Preferences on your iMac by Clicking on the Apple menu (□) in the upper-left corner of your screen and selecting **System Settings**.

Overview of Options: In System Preferences, you'll see various categories, such as **Network**, **Displays**, **Sound**, and **Security & Privacy**. Click on any category to explore its specific settings.

Search Functionality: You can use the search bar at the top right of the System Preferences window to quickly find a specific setting or preference.

For further customization, you can also manage user accounts, **parental controls**, and accessibility features within this section.

How to Customize the Control Center

The **Control Center** on macOS provides quick access to frequently used settings, similar to the feature on iOS devices. Here's how to customize it:

1. **Accessing Control Center**: Click the Control Center icon in the menu bar (it looks like two toggle switches). This will reveal a panel with various controls, such as Wi-Fi, Bluetooth, Display brightness, and Sound settings.

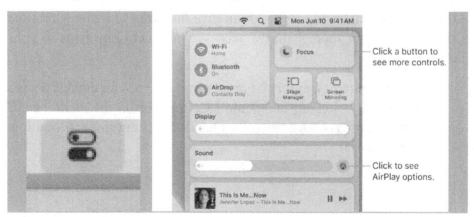

2. **Customizing the Control Center**:

Adding or Removing Items: To customize what appears in your Control Center, go back to **System Preferences** > **Control Center**. Here, you can choose which items to display, such as **Wi-Fi**, **Bluetooth**, **Do Not Disturb**, and **Screen Mirroring**. Simply drag and drop the items you want in or out of the Control Center.

Choose additional modules
to add to Control Center.

Organizing Items: You can also rearrange the order of items within the Control Center for more intuitive access. Click and drag items to your desired position.

3. **Using Control Center**: Once customized, you can quickly access settings by clicking the Control Center icon in the menu bar. It allows for easy adjustments without navigating through multiple menus.

Use Siri and Spotlight Search

The redesigned Siri helps users accelerate tasks throughout their day. Siri can be placed anywhere on the desktop for easy access, and with the option to type requests, users can get Siri's help in even a quiet space like an office.

Activating and Using Siri

Siri is Apple's virtual assistant that can help you perform a variety of tasks using voice commands. Here's how to activate and use Siri on your iMac:

Enable Siri: Go to **System Preferences** > **Siri**. Check the box next to **Enable Ask Siri**. You can choose to activate Siri using a keyboard.

Activate Siri: You can activate Siri by clicking the Siri icon in the menu bar or Dock, or by using the keyboard shortcut (usually Command + Space).

Once activated, you can ask Siri questions or give commands. For example, you can say:

- "What's the weather today?"
- "Open Safari."
- "Send a message to [Contact Name]."

Managing Siri Settings: In the Siri preferences, you can customize the voice, language, and feedback options, allowing for a more personalized experience.

Searching Files and Applications with Spotlight

Spotlight is a powerful search feature in macOS that allows you to quickly find files, applications, and information on your iMac. Here's how to use it effectively:

Activate Spotlight: Press Command + Spacebar to open the Spotlight search bar.

Type in the name of the file, application, or topic you want to search for. Spotlight will provide suggestions in real time as you type.

Start typing, and results appear quickly.

You can also search for web results, calculations, unit conversions, and even dictionary definitions.

Refining Searches: Use keywords to narrow down your search. For instance, typing "Documents" will show files in your Documents folder, while "Applications" will filter results to apps installed on your Mac.

Launching Applications: You can launch applications directly from Spotlight by typing the app's name and pressing Enter when it appears in the search results.

Both Siri and Spotlight Search significantly enhance the efficiency of your workflow on macOS, making it easy to access information and perform tasks quickly.

iMac Connectivity and Compatibility

Connecting Accessories and External Devices

The 2024 iMac with the M4 chip offers a variety of connectivity options that allow you to connect multiple accessories and external devices seamlessly.

Using USB-C, Thunderbolt, and Other Available Ports

1. **USB-C/Thunderbolt Ports**:

   o The Thunderbolt 4/USB-C ports provide high-speed data transfer and versatility. These ports are compatible with a wide range of devices, including external storage drives, displays, and docks.

   o **Thunderbolt 4** supports up to 40 Gbps transfer speeds and can daisy-chain up to six devices, making it ideal for high-performance peripherals and External Devices.

   o To connect a device, simply plug it into one of the available ports. If you are using a device with a different connector (like USB-A), you might need an adapter.

   o Ensure your device is compatible with Thunderbolt 4 for optimal performance. You can check the specifications on the manufacturer's website or the product box.

Connecting Storage, and Displays

Printers: You can connect a printer using USB-C or via your home network. For USB connections, plug the printer into a USB-C port. For wireless printers, go to **System Preferences** > **Printers & Scanners** to add your printer over Wi-Fi.

External Storage: Connect external hard drives or SSDs via Thunderbolt or USB-C ports. Once connected, you can access the drives through Finder, and they will appear on the desktop.

Displays: To connect an external monitor, use a Thunderbolt 4 cable. The iMac supports up to two external displays with up to 6K resolution at 60Hz. Go to **System Preferences** > **Displays** to configure the display settings.

Bluetooth Accessory Setup

Go to **System Preferences** > **Bluetooth** and ensure Bluetooth is turned on.

1. **Connecting AirPods or Bluetooth Speakers**:

Put your AirPods or Bluetooth speaker in pairing mode. For AirPods, open the case near your iMac and press the button on the back. For other devices, refer to the manufacturer's instructions. Your iMac will detect the device; click **Connect** when it appears in the Bluetooth menu.

2. **Managing Bluetooth Devices**:

Once connected manage and disconnect devices from the Bluetooth menu in System Preferences. Ensure your devices remain within range to maintain a stable connection.

Wi-Fi and Ethernet Setup

Setting up your iMac for internet connectivity is crucial for accessing online resources, apps, and services. Here's how to connect to a Wi-Fi network and set up an Ethernet connection for a wired setup.

1. **Open Wi-Fi Settings**:

Click the **Wi-Fi icon** in the menu bar at the top-right corner of your screen. If the Wi-Fi is off, select **Turn Wi-Fi On**.

2. **Choose a Network**:

After turning on Wi-Fi, a list of available networks will appear. Select your desired Wi-Fi network from the list.

3. **Enter Password**:

If the network is secured, you will be prompted to enter the Wi-Fi password. Type the password and click **Join**. Once connected, the Wi-Fi icon will indicate the signal strength.

4. **Confirm Connection**:

To confirm your connection, you can return to the Wi-Fi icon, which will now display the network name you are connected to. You can also check your connection in **System Preferences** > **Network**.

Setting Up Ethernet for a Wired Connection

1. **Connect Ethernet Cable**:

Plug one end of an Ethernet cable into the iMac's Ethernet port or use a Thunderbolt to Ethernet adapter if necessary. Connect the other end to your router or modem.

2. **Open Network Settings**:

Click on the Apple menu (□) > **System Preferences** > **Network**.

3. **Select Ethernet**:

In the left panel, select **Ethernet** from the list of connections. If it's not listed, click the + button to add a new connection and select **Ethernet**.

4. **Configure Settings**:

Your iMac should automatically detect the Ethernet connection and configure the settings. If you need to enter a manual IP address or configure additional settings, select **Advanced** to make adjustments.

5. **Confirm Connection**:

Once connected, the status should show as "Connected" with the IP address displayed. You can check internet connectivity by opening a web browser.

Setting up both Wi-Fi and Ethernet connections ensures a reliable internet experience, whether you're in a location with good Wi-Fi or prefer the stability of a wired connection.

Screen Mirroring and AirPlay

With AirPlay, your iMac allows you to mirror or extend your display to compatible Apple devices like an Apple TV, another Mac, or select smart TVs. Here's how to use AirPlay for screen mirroring or dual-screen setups.

How to Use AirPlay

Make sure the devices you want to use AirPlay with are compatible. AirPlay works with Apple TV. AirPlay-enabled TVs, and other recent Apple devices like iPhones, iPads, and Macs.

1. **Enable AirPlay on Your iMac**:

In the **Control Center** (located in the menu bar), select **Screen Mirroring**. This option allows you to choose from available devices to mirror your display.

2. **Select Your Device**:

When you click **Screen Mirroring**, a list of available AirPlay devices will appear. Select the device you want to mirror to, such as an Apple TV or another Mac. The display will automatically start mirroring on the selected device.

3. **Adjust Settings**:

For more control, go to **System Preferences** > **Displays** > **AirPlay Display**. Here, you can fine-tune options like resolution, display arrangement, and audio preferences if you're using AirPlay for sound as well.

Setting Up Dual-Screen or Mirrored Display Option

1. **Mirror vs. Extend Display**:

Mirrored Display: This duplicates your iMac's screen on another device.

Extended Display: This option expands your desktop across two screens, allowing you to use one screen as a continuation of the other.

2. **Activating Dual-Screen or Mirrored Mode**:

Open **System Preferences** > **Displays**. Under the **Arrangement** tab, you can arrange the screens by dragging them or toggle **Mirror Displays** to replicate your iMac screen on the second display.

3. **Adjust Display Arrangement**:

To organize your dual-screen setup, click and drag the screens in **Display Arrangement** to your preferred layout. This layout affects cursor movement and app window placement.

These features make it easy to use multiple displays for productivity or entertainment purposes.

BUILT-IN APPS AND UTILITIES

Safari Web Browser

Safari is Apple's powerful and privacy-focused web browser, known for its speed and integration with the macOS ecosystem. The 2024 iMac with the M4 chip takes advantage of Safari's newest features, improving browsing experience and productivity.

New Features in Safari

1. **Redesigned Tab Groups**:

Tab Groups have been improved, allowing you to organize tabs into groups for different projects or interests. These groups can sync across your devices via iCloud, so you can access them from any Apple device. You can now pin tabs within Tab Groups for quick access to important pages.

2. **Passkeys and Enhanced Password Management**:

Safari's built-in password manager now includes Passkeys, Apple's passwordless login option that enhances security by removing the need for traditional passwords. Passkeys sync securely across your devices, and you can manage them directly in Safari's settings.

3. **Improved Privacy Protection**:

Safari now features enhanced privacy settings, including improved Intelligent Tracking Prevention, which blocks even more trackers from gathering data across websites. Safari also provides detailed reports on blocked trackers to keep you informed.

4. **Enhanced Performance with M4 Optimization**:

Safari's performance is further enhanced with the M4 chip's processing capabilities. Loading times are faster, and there's optimized battery life for longer browsing sessions.

Managing Bookmarks and Browsing History

1. **Adding and Organizing Bookmarks**:

To bookmark a page, simply click the **Share** icon (a square with an arrow) in the toolbar and select **Add Bookmark**. You can organize bookmarks into folders by accessing the **Bookmarks Sidebar** (click the **Sidebar** icon or use Command + Shift + B).

To create folders, right-click in the Bookmarks Sidebar and select **New Folder**. Drag and drop bookmarks into folders for organization.

2. **Browsing History**:

Safari automatically keeps track of your browsing history. To access it, go to **History** in the menu bar. From here, you can view or clear your history. For more selective deletion, click **Show All History** and remove specific entries.

Using Tabs and Tab Groups

1. **Managing Tabs**:

Open new tabs by pressing Command + T or by clicking the + icon in the tab bar. Safari supports tab pinning, where you can right-click on a tab and select **Pin Tab** to keep frequently used tabs accessible and reduce clutter.

2. **Creating and Using Tab Groups**:

Click on the **Sidebar** icon, select **Tab Groups**, and then click **New Empty Tab Group** or **New Tab Group with [X] Tabs** to group your open tabs.

You can rename, reorder, or delete Tab Groups from the Sidebar. These groups sync with other Apple devices, allowing seamless transitions between your iMac and other devices.

Mail, Calendar, and Contacts

Setting Up Email Accounts in Mail

1. **Open the Mail App**:

Launch the Mail app by clicking the **Mail** icon in your dock or searching for it using Spotlight (Command + Space).

2. **Add an Email Account**:

Go to **Mail** in the menu bar, select **Add Account**, and choose your email provider (like iCloud, Gmail, or Outlook). For custom domains, select **Other Mail Account** and enter your email details manually.

3. **Sign In and Customize Settings**:

After signing in, you can customize email settings, such as sync frequency and notification preferences, through **Mail** > **Settings** > **Accounts**.

4. **Organize Mailboxes and Folders**:

You can create custom mailboxes and folders to organize emails. Right-click in the mailbox sidebar to create new folders and drag emails into them.

Adding Events to the Calendar

1. **Open the Calendar App**:

Open **Calendar** from the dock or via Spotlight search.

2. **Create a New Event**:

Double-click on the desired date, or click the + icon to add an event. Enter event details, including the title, location, and time. You can also add notes, attachments, and links for more context.

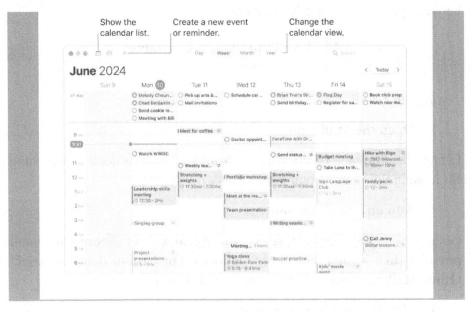

3. **Set Reminders and Alerts**:

Configure reminders by selecting **Alert** in the event details, which allows you to receive notifications on your iMac and synced devices.

4. **Syncing with Other Calendars**:

To sync other calendars (Google, Outlook, etc.), go to **Calendar** > **Accounts** and add your account details. This will sync events across devices and platforms, keeping everything updated in real-time.

Managing Contacts and Syncing with Other Devices

1. **Open Contacts App**:

Launch the **Contacts** app from the dock or via Spotlight. This app stores all your contacts and integrates with Mail and Calendar for easy access.

2. **Add and Edit Contacts**:

Click the + button to create a new contact. You can enter details like phone numbers, email addresses, and notes. To edit an existing contact, simply double-click on their name.

3. **Syncing Contacts Across Devices**:

Go to **Contacts** > **Accounts** and add accounts (such as iCloud, Google, or Microsoft) to sync contacts from other devices. Ensure **Contacts** sync is enabled in **System Preferences** > **Apple ID** for iCloud contacts, or through the specific account settings for third-party services.

These built-in apps integrate seamlessly, providing a unified workspace to manage emails, events, and contacts.

Messages and FaceTime

Setting Up and Use Messages

1. **Open the Messages App**:

Launch the **Messages** app by clicking on its icon in the dock or by searching for it with Spotlight.

Enter search
criteria.

Click to create
a new message.

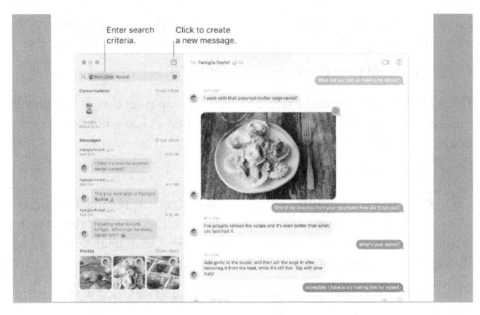

2. **Sign In with Apple ID**:

When you open Messages for the first time, you'll be prompted to sign in with your **Apple ID**. Enter your credentials to connect your iMessage account.

Manage a conversation, share
your location, and more.

Click to add photos, schedule
a message, and more.

3. **Sync Messages Across Devices**:

To ensure that messages are synced between your iMac and other Apple devices (iPhone, iPad, etc.), go to **Messages** > **Settings** > **iMessage**. Enable **Messages in iCloud** to sync conversations across devices.

4. **Send and Receive Messages**:

Click the **New Message** icon to start a conversation, enter the contact's name, email, or phone number, and type your message. Messages sent to other Apple devices via iMessage will appear in blue, while SMS messages will appear in green if you're synced with an iPhone.

5. **Using Effects and Attachments**:

Messages on iMac support rich features like sending photos, and videos, and using fun effects. Click on the **Apps** icon next to the text box to add images or effects.

FaceTime Calls and Configuring Settings

1. **Open FaceTime App**:

Open **FaceTime** from your dock or via Spotlight search.

2. **Sign In and Configure Settings**:

When you launch FaceTime for the first time, you'll be prompted to sign in with your **Apple ID**. You can configure settings by going to

FaceTime > **Settings**, where you can set your caller ID, enable FaceTime Live Photos, and manage notification preferences.

3. **Making a FaceTime Call**:

To make a FaceTime call, enter the contact's name, email, or phone number in the FaceTime app. You can select **Audio** or **Video** depending on the type of call you want to make.

4. **Using FaceTime with Multiple Participants**:

With FaceTime, you can start a Group FaceTime call with up to 32 participants. Simply add multiple contacts in the **To** field before starting the call.

5. **Integration with Messages**:

FaceTime is integrated with the Messages app. From an ongoing iMessage conversation, you can quickly start a FaceTime call by clicking on the contact's name at the top and selecting **FaceTime**.

Photos and Files Apps

Importing and Organizing Photos

1. **Open the Photos App**:

Start by opening the **Photos** app from your dock or via Spotlight. The Photos app organizes your pictures and videos, making it easy to sort, edit, and view your media files.

2. **Importing Photos**:

To import photos from an external device (like a camera or iPhone), connect the device to your iMac. In the Photos app, click **File** > **Import**, then select the photos you want to import. You can also drag and drop photos directly into the Photos library.

If iCloud Photos is enabled, your iCloud photo library will sync automatically across all Apple devices.

3. **Organizing Photos**:

Photos organize media by **Moments**, **Collections**, and **Years** for a timeline view, while **Albums** lets you create custom groups.

Use **Favourites** to mark your most-loved photos, or try the **People** and **Places** features to categorize by faces or locations. The **Search** function allows you to look for photos by date, location, or even object recognition.

4. **Editing Tools**:

Photos offer basic editing options, like cropping, filters, and adjustments to brightness, contrast, and colour. To edit, select a photo and click **Edit**. Your changes sync across devices if iCloud Photos is on, and edits are non-destructive, meaning you can revert to the original anytime.

Using the Files App

1. **Open the Files App**:

On macOS, the equivalent of the Files app is **Finder**, which manages all your documents, applications, downloads, and folders.

2. **Navigating and Organizing Files**:

Finder organizes files under **Locations** (such as iCloud Drive, external drives, or Network drives) and **Favourites** (including Desktop, Documents, and Downloads).

To organize files, drag them into folders, or right-click to create new folders and label them. You can also add **Tags** to files for easy searching, which helps group files by project or theme.

3. **Searching and Quick Look**:

Use the **Search bar** at the top of Finder to locate files quickly, or press the **Spacebar** for **Quick Look** to preview documents without fully opening them.

4. **Managing iCloud Drive and External Storage**:

iCloud Drive allows you to store documents in the cloud and access them across Apple devices. To manage, go to **Finder** > **Preferences** > **Sidebar** and enable iCloud Drive.

For external storage, connect your device and access it from the **Locations** section in Finder. Drag and drop files between your iMac and external drives to transfer data.

PRODUCTIVITY TOOLS

Using iWork Suite

The iWork Suite consists of three primary applications: **Pages**, **Numbers**, and **Keynote**. These tools provide powerful yet user-friendly options for creating documents, spreadsheets, and presentations.

1. **Getting Started with Pages**:

Open the **Pages** app from your dock or via Spotlight. Upon launching, you can choose from various templates or create a blank document.

2. **Creating and Formatting Documents**:

Use the toolbar at the top to format text (fonts, sizes, styles) and insert images, tables, and shapes. The **Format** sidebar allows for detailed adjustments, such as alignment and spacing.

To collaborate in real-time, use **Share** in the toolbar, which enables you to invite others to edit or view the document online via iCloud.

3. **Exporting Documents**:

Once your document is ready, export it by clicking **File** > **Export To**, allowing you to save it in various formats (PDF, Word, etc.).

Getting Started with Numbers for Spreadsheets

1. **Opening Numbers**:

Launch **Numbers** from your dock or via Spotlight. Like Pages, it offers several templates tailored for budgets, financial reports, and project tracking.

2. **Creating Spreadsheets**:

You can easily input data into cells, create formulas, and visualize data using charts. The **Format** sidebar provides options for cell formatting and chart styles.

3. **Collaboration and Sharing**:

Use the **Share** button to collaborate with others in real time or to send a copy of your spreadsheet via email or iCloud.

4. **Exporting Spreadsheets**:

To export your finished spreadsheet, go to **File** > **Export To** and select your desired file format.

Keynote for Presentations

1. **Starting Keynote**:

Open **Keynote** from your dock or via Spotlight, and select a template that suits your presentation style.

2. **Creating and Designing Presentations**:

Add slides, images, and text using the toolbar. You can customize transitions and animations to enhance the visual appeal of your presentation.

3. **Collaboration Features**:

Similar to Pages and Numbers, you can collaborate with others by clicking on the **Collaborate** button. This allows multiple users to work on the presentation simultaneously.

4. **Presenting and Exporting**:

When ready to present, use the **Play** button to start. To export your presentation, select **File** > **Export To** and choose a suitable format (PDF, PowerPoint, etc.).

The iWork Suite provides a robust set of tools to enhance productivity on your iMac, enabling you to create professional-quality documents, spreadsheets, and presentations with ease.

Notes, Reminders, and Apple Music

How to Organize Information with Notes

1. **Opening the Notes App**:

Launch the **Notes** app from your dock or by searching via Spotlight. You'll find a clean interface where you can start organizing your thoughts and ideas.

2. **Creating Notes**:

Click the **New Note** button (represented by a pencil and paper icon) to start a new entry. You can format text, create checklists, add images, and even sketch using the drawing tools available in the toolbar.

3. **Organizing Your Notes**:

Utilize **Folders** to categorize your notes. Click **Folders** on the left sidebar and select **New Folder** to create one. You can drag and drop notes into these folders for better organization.

Use the **Search** function at the top of the Notes app to quickly find specific entries based on keywords or tags.

4. **Collaborating on Notes**:

You can share notes with others by clicking the **Share** button. This allows for real-time collaboration, enabling multiple users to edit the same note.

Setting Reminders and To-Dos

Opening the Reminders App: Access the **Reminders** app from your dock or via Spotlight. The interface is straightforward and designed for easy task management.

1. **Creating Reminders**:

Click on **New Reminder** to enter your task. You can set specific due dates, locations, and priority levels by clicking on the **i** icon next to each reminder.

Organizing Tasks: You can create **Lists** within Reminders to categorize your tasks (e.g., Work, Personal, Shopping). Simply click **Add List** at the bottom and give it a name. To keep track of recurring tasks, select the **Repeat** option while setting up a reminder.

Collaboration and Sharing: Share your reminders list with others by clicking **Add People**. This allows shared access and collaboration on tasks.

Apple Music and Connecting to HomePod

Opening Apple Music: Launch the **Apple Music** app from your dock. If you're a subscriber, you can access an extensive library of songs, playlists, and curated content.

Navigating Apple Music: Explore different sections like **Listen Now**, **Browse**, and **Library**. You can search for specific songs or artists using the search bar at the top.

Creating Playlists: To create a playlist, go to the **Library** section, select **Playlists**, and click **New Playlist**. You can add songs from your library or Apple Music.

Connecting to HomePod: Ensure your HomePod is set up on the same Wi-Fi network as your iMac. In Apple Music, click on the **AirPlay** icon and select your HomePod from the list to stream music wirelessly. You can control playback and volume through your iMac or by using voice commands with Siri on your HomePod.

Siri: Say something like: "Continue playing the last podcast."

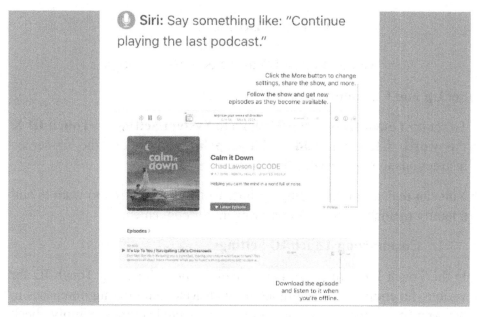

These applications enhance your productivity and entertainment experience on the iMac.

ADVANCED FEATURES

Using Touch ID and Security Settings

Set Up and Customize Touch ID

To set up **Touch ID** on your iMac, go to **System Settings** > **Touch ID & Password**. Click on **Add a Fingerprint** and follow the on-screen instructions to register your fingerprint.

You can register multiple fingerprints, which is useful if you want to add a family member or use different fingers for convenience.

1. **Customizing Touch ID Settings**:

In the Touch ID settings, you can enable options for using Touch ID for various functions, such as unlocking your Mac, authorizing purchases in the App Store, and accessing password-protected settings. Simply check or uncheck the relevant options to customize how Touch ID works for you.

2. **Managing Registered Fingerprints**:

If you need to delete a fingerprint or add a new one, go back to the **Touch ID & Password** settings. You can remove fingerprints by clicking on them and selecting **Delete**.

Manage Security and Privacy Settings

1. **Accessing Security & Privacy Settings**:

Open **System Settings** from the Apple menu, then click on **Privacy & Security**. Here, you can control various security settings that protect your iMac.

2. **Configuring General Security Settings**:

In the **General** tab, you can set preferences for requiring a password after sleep or screen saver activation, enabling FileVault for disk encryption, and managing your firewall settings. Make sure to keep your firewall enabled for added protection against unauthorized access.

3. **Privacy Controls**:

Under the **Privacy** tab, you can manage which applications have access to your location, contacts, calendar, photos, and more. Regularly review these settings to ensure that only trusted apps have access to sensitive information.

4. **Managing App Permissions**:

Click on **Camera**, **Microphone**, and **Accessibility** in the Privacy section to see which apps have requested permission. You can enable or disable these permissions based on your preferences.

5. **Software Updates**:

Keeping your system up-to-date is crucial for security. Go to **Software Update** under **System Settings** to check for and install the latest macOS updates, which often include important security patches.

Multi-Tasking Features

Split-Screen, Mission Control, and Spaces

1. **Using Split Screen**:

Split View allows you to run two applications side by side. To enter Split View, open the first app, then click and hold the green full-screen button in the upper-left corner. Drag the window to either side of the screen, then select a second app to fill the other half. This is ideal for comparing documents or multitasking effectively. You can exit Split View by pressing the escape key or clicking the green button again.

2. **Mission Control**:

Mission Control provides an overview of all open windows and desktops. To activate Mission Control, swipe up with three or four fingers on the trackpad, or press the **F3** key (or Control + Up Arrow). From here, you can easily switch between apps, manage open windows, and access your Desktop or Spaces.

You can create additional desktops (Spaces) by moving your cursor to the top right corner of your screen in Mission Control and clicking the + button. This helps you organize different workflows, such as work and personal tasks, on separate desktops.

3. **Spaces**:

Spaces are virtual desktops that allow you to organize your workspace. You can switch between Spaces using Mission Control or by swiping left or right with three fingers on the trackpad. This feature is useful for keeping related applications and tasks grouped together, enhancing focus and productivity.

Using the Universal Clipboard

1. **What is a Universal Clipboard?**

The **Universal Clipboard** feature allows you to copy text, images, and other content from one Apple device and paste it on another. For example, you can copy text on your iPhone and paste it directly into a document on your iMac, as long as both devices are signed in to the same Apple ID and have Bluetooth and Wi-Fi enabled.

Your calls and texts come right to your iMac, so you don't need to switch devices when you're in the zone.

And you can use your iPhone to take a picture or scan a document and have it automatically appear on your iMac.

2. **How to Use Universal Clipboard**:

To use this feature, simply copy the desired content on your first device (using the usual copy command), then switch to your iMac and use the paste command. The copied content should appear seamlessly.

Ensure that **Handoff** is enabled on both devices. Go to **System Settings** > **General** > **AirPlay & Handoff** on your iMac, and toggle on Handoff. On your iPhone or iPad, go to **Settings** > **General** > **AirPlay & Handoff**.

3. **Troubleshooting**:

If the Universal Clipboard doesn't work, ensure both devices are within Bluetooth range, Wi-Fi is active, and you're signed into the same iCloud account. Restarting both devices can also help resolve issues.

Accessibility Settings

iMac for Different Accessibility Needs

To customize accessibility features, go to **System Settings** > **Accessibility**. There are various tools designed to assist users with different needs, making your iMac more user-friendly.

1. **Setting Up Accessibility Options**:

You can enable features that cater to specific needs, such as adjusting the display, enhancing audio, or providing text-to-speech options. Customization allows users to tailor their experience according to individual requirements.

2. **Keyboard and Mouse Adjustments**:

Modify the keyboard settings to include options like Sticky Keys, Slow Keys, and Mouse Keys. These settings can help those who may have difficulty using standard keyboard functions.

VoiceOver

What is VoiceOver?: VoiceOver is a built-in screen reader that provides spoken descriptions of what is on your screen. This feature enables visually impaired users to navigate their iMac effectively.

- **Enabling VoiceOver**:

To activate VoiceOver, go to **Accessibility** settings and select **VoiceOver**. You can turn it on by checking the box or using the keyboard shortcut **Command + F5**.

- **Customizing VoiceOver Settings**:

VoiceOver offers a variety of customization options, including voice selection, speech rate, and verbosity settings. You can also practice using the VoiceOver cursor to navigate your iMac intuitively.

Zoom

What is Zoom?: Zoom is a screen magnification feature that allows users to enlarge content on the screen for better visibility. It's particularly useful for users with low vision.

- **Enabling Zoom**:

Go to **Accessibility** > **Zoom** in System Settings. You can turn on the zoom feature and customize the zoom level and style (full-screen or picture-in-picture).

- **Using Zoom**:

Once enabled, you can zoom in and out using keyboard shortcuts or by holding down the **Control** key while scrolling with your mouse or trackpad.

Other Accessibility Options

1. **Display Adjustments**:

Users can enhance visibility by adjusting the display settings, such as increasing contrast, reducing transparency, and inverting colours. These features help users with visual impairments better see screen content.

2. **Hearing Accessibility**:

The accessibility settings also include options for users with hearing impairments, such as enabling closed captions and customizing audio settings to better suit individual needs.

3. **AssistiveTouch**:

This feature allows users with motor difficulties to use gestures and shortcuts to navigate their iMac, making it easier to access various functions without needing traditional input devices.

These accessibility settings and features make the iMac usable for everyone, ensuring that users with diverse needs can comfortably operate their devices.

CUSTOMIZATION AND PERSONALIZATION

Display Settings

Adjusting Screen Brightness and Resolution

Screen Brightness: To adjust the screen brightness on your iMac, you can use the keyboard shortcuts: the F1 key decreases brightness and the F2 key increases it. Alternatively, you can go to **System Settings** > **Displays** and manually adjust the brightness slider for precise control.

Screen Resolution: The iMac supports various screen resolutions. To change the resolution, navigate to **System Settings** > **Displays**. Here, you can choose **Default for Display** or **Scaled** options to select a resolution that best fits your needs. Selecting a higher resolution provides sharper text and images, while lower resolutions can make items larger and easier to see.

Refresh Rate: If your iMac supports it, you can also adjust the refresh rate in the **Displays** settings under **Resolution**. Higher refresh rates provide smoother motion, which is particularly beneficial for gaming and video playback.

Enabling True Tone and Night Shift

True Tone: True Tone technology adjusts the white balance of your display according to the ambient lighting conditions, ensuring that images appear more natural. To enable True Tone, go to **System Settings** > **Displays** and check the box next to **True Tone**.

Night Shift: Night Shift reduces blue light exposure by shifting the colours of your display to the warmer end of the spectrum during the evening. To enable Night Shift, go to **System Settings** > **Displays** > **Night**

Shift. You can schedule it to turn on automatically from sunset to sunrise or set a custom time range.

Adjusting Night Shift Settings: In the Night Shift settings, you can adjust the colour temperature to your preference (More Warm or Less Warm) to find the most comfortable viewing experience.

Keyboard, Mouse, and Trackpad Settings

Customizing Keyboard Shortcuts

Accessing Keyboard Shortcuts: To customize keyboard shortcuts on your iMac, go to **System Settings** > **Keyboard** and click on the **Keyboard Shortcuts** tab. Here, you will find a list of all available shortcuts organized by categories such as Mission Control, App Shortcuts, and Accessibility.

Creating Custom Shortcuts: You can create your own keyboard shortcuts for specific applications or system functions. Click the **App Shortcuts** option, then click the + button to add a new shortcut. Select the application, type the exact name of the menu command you want to create a shortcut for and choose your desired key combination.

Shortcuts are built with a series of actions.

Click to run the shortcut.

Choose actions in the Action Library.

Resetting Shortcuts: If you wish to reset your keyboard shortcuts to their default settings, you can do so by clicking the **Restore Defaults** button in the Keyboard Shortcuts menu.

Adjusting Mouse Speed and Gestures

Mouse Speed: To adjust the mouse speed, go to **System Settings** > **Mouse**. Here, you can find the **Tracking speed** slider, which allows you to customize how quickly the pointer moves in response to your mouse movements.

Mouse Gestures: If you're using a Magic Mouse, you can enable and customize gestures in the **Mouse** settings. For instance, you can use gestures for swiping between pages, scrolling through documents, or accessing Mission Control.

Gesture	Action
	Turn on/off: Slide the on/off switch on the bottom of the mouse to turn it on (so green is visible).
	Click: Press the upper surface of the mouse to click or double-click.
	Secondary click (that is, right-click): Press the left or right side of the mouse to perform a "secondary click." (To enable right- and left-click, in System Settings, click Mouse, then select "Secondary click.") Or press the Control key on the keyboard as you click the mouse.
	360° scroll: Brush one finger along the surface to scroll or pan in any direction.
	360° scroll: Brush one finger along the surface to scroll or pan in any direction.
	Screen zoom: Hold down the Control key and scroll with one finger to enlarge items on the screen. (To enable screen zoom, in System Settings, click Accessibility, click Zoom, then select "Use scroll gesture with modifier keys to zoom.")
	Two-finger swipe: Swipe left or right to move through pages, photos, and more.

1. **Trackpad Settings:**

If you are using a trackpad, navigate to **System Settings** > **Trackpad**. Here, you can adjust tracking speed and enable features such as **Tap to click**, **Secondary click**, and various gestures (like pinch to zoom and swipe between full-screen apps).

Gesture	Action		
●	Click: Press anywhere on the trackpad. Or enable "Tap to click" in Trackpad settings, and simply tap.		Pinch to zoom: Pinch your thumb and finger open or closed to zoom in or out of photos and webpages.
◎	Force click: Click and then press deeper. You can use force click to look up more information—click a word to see its definition, or an address to see a preview that you can open in Maps.		Swipe to navigate: Swipe left or right with two fingers to flip through webpages, documents, and more—like turning a page in a book.
● ●	Secondary click (that is, right-click): Click with two fingers to open shortcut menus. If "Tap to click" is enabled, tap or click with two fingers. Or press the Control key on the keyboard as you click the trackpad.		Open Launchpad: Quickly open apps in Launchpad. Pinch closed with four or five fingers, then click an app to open it.
⇡⇣	Two-finger scroll: Slide two fingers up or down to scroll.		Swipe between apps: To switch from one full-screen app to another, swipe left or right with three or four fingers.

2. **Gesture Customization**:

In the Trackpad settings, you can also enable or disable specific gestures based on your preference, ensuring that your workflow is as smooth and efficient as possible.

Notifications and Focus Modes

Managing App Notifications

1. **Accessing Notification Settings**:

To manage your notifications, go to **System Settings** > **Notifications**. Here, you will see a list of all your installed apps and their current notification settings.

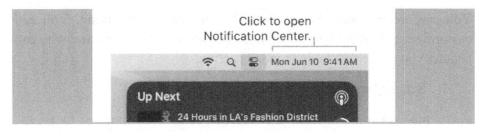

2. Customizing Notifications:

For each app, you can choose how you want to receive notifications. Options include allowing notifications, showing them in the Notification Center, and setting alerts to appear as banners or alerts. You can also customize the sounds associated with notifications.

3. Disabling Unwanted Notifications:

If you find certain apps are sending too many notifications, you can easily turn them off by selecting the app and toggling off the option to allow notifications.

4. Using Do Not Disturb:

You can temporarily silence all notifications by enabling **Do Not Disturb** from the Notifications settings. This is helpful when you need uninterrupted time to focus on your work.

Setting Up Focus Modes for Better Productivity

1. Accessing Focus Modes:

Focus modes allow you to customize your notification settings based on your current activity (work, personal time, sleep, etc.). To set up Focus modes, go to **System Settings** > **Focus**.

2. Creating a New Focus Mode:

You can create a new Focus mode by clicking the + button. You can customize settings such as which apps can send notifications and who can contact you while that Focus mode is active.

3. **Scheduling Focus Modes**:

Focus modes can be scheduled to activate at specific times or locations. For example, you might want your Work Focus to turn on during office hours automatically.

4. **Syncing Across Devices**:

When you set up a Focus mode, it can sync across all your Apple devices (iPhone, iPad, etc.) if you're using the same Apple ID. This way, you maintain your desired focus level regardless of the device you're using.

5. **Focus Status**:

You can enable **Focus Status**, which lets others know you have notifications silenced. This feature can help minimize interruptions when working or engaging in personal time.

TROUBLESHOOTING AND MAINTENANCE

Basic Troubleshooting

What to Do If the iMac Doesn't Turn On

1. **Check Power Connection**:

Ensure that the power cable is securely connected to both the iMac and the electrical outlet. Sometimes, a loose connection can prevent the iMac from turning on. If using a power strip, ensure it is switched on.

2. **Perform a Power Cycle**:

Unplug the power cord, wait for at least 15 seconds, and then plug it back in. After that, press the power button to see if the iMac turns on.

3. **Reset SMC (System Management Controller)**:

If your iMac is still unresponsive, you might need to reset the SMC. Shut down your iMac, unplug the power cord, wait 15 seconds, plug it back in, and then turn on the iMac. This can resolve power-related issues.

4. **Check for External Devices**:

Disconnect any peripherals (like external drives, printers, etc.) to rule out issues caused by connected devices. Then try powering on the iMac again.

Resolving Connectivity Issues:

Check Wi-Fi Status: Make sure Wi-Fi is enabled. Go to **System Settings** > **Network** to verify that your Wi-Fi is connected.

Restart Router: Sometimes, the issue lies with the router. Restart your router and try reconnecting.

Forget and Rejoin Network: If you continue to have issues, you can forget the network by going to **System Settings** > **Network** > **Wi-Fi**.

Click on **Advanced,** select the network, and click the - button. Reconnect by selecting the network and entering the password.

Bluetooth Connection Issues:

Turn Bluetooth Off and On: Go to **System Settings > Bluetooth** and toggle Bluetooth off and back on to refresh the connection.

Check Device Compatibility: Ensure that the Bluetooth device you are trying to connect is compatible with your iMac.

Remove and Re-Pair Devices: If a Bluetooth device isn't connecting, remove it from the list in Bluetooth settings and then attempt to re-pair it by putting the device into pairing mode.

These troubleshooting steps should help you resolve common issues with your 2024 iMac. If problems persist, you may need to contact Apple Support or visit an Apple Store for assistance.

Resetting and Restoring the iMac

Performing a Factory Reset

1. **Back-Up Your Data**:

Before resetting your iMac, ensure you back up any important data. You can use Time Machine to create a backup.

2. **Restart the iMac**:

Click on the **Apple menu** in the top-left corner and select **Restart**.

3. **Enter Recovery Mode**:

Immediately after the iMac restarts, hold down **Command (⌘) + R** until you see the Apple logo or a spinning globe. This will boot your iMac into Recovery Mode.

4. **Erase the Hard Drive**:

Once in Recovery Mode, select **Disk Utility** from the macOS Utilities window, then click **Continue**.

In Disk Utility, select your startup disk (usually named "Macintosh HD") from the sidebar and click on the **Erase** button. Choose the format (APFS is recommended for SSDs) and confirm the action.

5. **Reinstall macOS**:

After erasing the disk, return to the macOS Utilities window and select **Reinstall macOS**. Follow the on-screen instructions to reinstall the operating system.

6. **Complete Setup**:

Once the installation is complete, your iMac will restart. Follow the setup prompts to configure your iMac as new or restore from a backup.

Back-Up and Restore Data Using Time Machine

1. **Setting Up Time Machine**:

Connect an external hard drive to your iMac. You can use a drive specifically formatted for Time Machine (APFS or Mac OS Extended).

Go to **System Settings** > **Time Machine** and select the external drive as your backup disk. Turn on the Time Machine to start automatic backups.

2. **Backing Up Your Data**:

Time Machine will automatically back up your data every hour, but you can also initiate a backup manually by clicking on the Time Machine icon in the menu bar and selecting **Back Up Now**.

3. **Restoring Data**:

To restore files from Time Machine, open the folder where the files were located. Click the **Time Machine** icon in the menu bar and select **Enter Time Machine**.

Navigate through the timeline on the right side to find the version of the file you want to restore. Select the file and click **Restore** to bring it back to its original location.

4. **Restoring the Entire System**:

If you are setting up your iMac after a factory reset and want to restore everything from a Time Machine backup, during the setup process, you can select **Restore from Time Machine Backup** and follow the prompts to complete the restoration.

Cleaning and Maintaining the iMac

1. **Gather Cleaning Supplies**:

Use a microfiber cloth, which is soft and non-abrasive, to prevent scratches on the screen.

For a cleaning solution, you can use a mix of 70% isopropyl alcohol and water, or opt for a screen-safe cleaner specifically designed for electronics. Avoid using window cleaners or any solution containing ammonia.

2. **Cleaning the Screen**:

First, power off the iMac and unplug it. This helps prevent any electrical issues and allows for better visibility of smudges.

Lightly dampen the microfiber cloth with the cleaning solution—do not spray it directly onto the screen.

Gently wipe the screen in circular motions to remove fingerprints and dust. Avoid applying excessive pressure.

3. **Cleaning the Body**:

Use a clean, dry microfiber cloth to wipe down the exterior of the iMac. If there are stubborn stains, lightly dampen the cloth with the cleaning solution and then wipe.

For the ports and keyboard, use a dry brush or compressed air to remove dust and debris, being careful not to damage the components.

Maintenance Practices for Optimal Performance

Keep your macOS and applications up to date to benefit from performance improvements and security patches.

Regularly check your storage usage and remove unnecessary files. You can use the **Storage Management** tool found in **About This Mac** > **Storage** > **Manage** to help identify large files and optimize space.

Use the built-in Disk Utility to check and repair your disk. Open **Disk Utility**, select your startup disk and click **First Aid** to run repairs on any disk errors.

Use the **Activity Monitor** app to track CPU, memory, and energy usage. If you notice any apps consuming excessive resources, consider closing them or troubleshooting. Ensure that your iMac is placed in a well-**ventilated area** to avoid overheating. Periodically check that the air vents are not obstructed and keep the environment **dust-free**. Use a Time Machine or another backup method to regularly back up your data. This ensures you don't lose important files due to hardware issues..

M4 Pro and M4 Max Chips

Apple also, recently introduced the **M4 Pro** and **M4 Max** chips, joining the M4 to create the most advanced chip lineup for personal computers. Built on second-generation 3-nanometer technology, these chips offer high power efficiency and impressive performance, featuring the fastest CPU core with industry-leading single and multithreaded processing. They include enhanced GPUs with a 2x faster ray-tracing engine, support for Thunderbolt 5, and a Neural Engine that's up to twice as fast, optimizing pro and AI workloads. These advancements are pushing Mac performance to new heights in power-efficient, privacy-focused computing.

The new M4 chip delivers exceptional performance to Mac, catering to entrepreneurs, students, and creators with a 10-core CPU and 10-core GPU that's up to 1.8x faster than M1, making multitasking and graphics-intensive tasks swift and smooth.

Supporting up to 32GB unified memory and Thunderbolt 4, M4 is optimized for high productivity. M4 Pro builds on this with a 14-core CPU, up to 20 GPU cores, support for Thunderbolt 5, and 64GB memory with 273GB/s bandwidth. It offers pro users, like developers and engineers, advanced capabilities for high-performance tasks, including AI, 3D rendering, and large file handling, with impressive power efficiency.

The M4 Max chip, designed for power users like data scientists and 3D artists, features a 16-core CPU and a 40-core GPU, delivering speeds up to 2.2x faster than M1 Max and up to 4x faster than top AI PC chips. It supports up to 128GB of memory with 546GB/s bandwidth, ideal for handling massive datasets and media tasks. Alongside powerful video encoding and ProRes support, M4 Max supports Thunderbolt 5, providing exceptional data transfer. Apple's "Apple Intelligence" in M4 chips enhances tasks with systemwide Writing Tools, Siri, and privacy-first on-device processing. Apple's commitment to energy efficiency contributes to reduced environmental impact, aligning with its 2030 carbon neutrality goal

Models of iMac M4

The 2024 iMac lineup with the new M4 chip includes two models: a base model and a higher-end version. Both models share a 24-inch display, come in seven colours, and feature Apple's advanced 10-core GPU and a 16-core Neural Engine capable of performing up to 38 trillion operations per second.

iMac with M4 features the world's fastest CPU core, making multitasking across apps like Safari and Excel lightning fast.

Key Differences:

Port Configuration: The base model has two Thunderbolt 4 ports, while the higher-end model includes four Thunderbolt 4 ports, offering expanded connectivity options

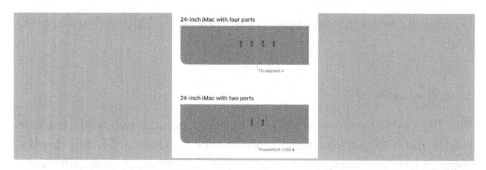

Memory and Storage: The base model starts with 16GB of unified memory and 256GB of storage, priced at around $1,299. In contrast, the upgraded model allows for 32GB of memory and up to 512GB of storage for approximately $1,699.

.Additional Features:

The higher-end model includes gigabit Ethernet and a Magic Keyboard with Touch ID for added security, whereas these features are optional for the base version.

Differences Between iMac with M4 and Previous M3 Version

The 2024 iMac with the M4 chips is upgraded over the M3 model. Key improvements include **faster processing speeds**, especially in productivity tasks, with up to 32GB of RAM (compared to 24GB in the M3) and increased **memory bandwidth** of 120GB/s. The M4 iMac also has improved **external display support**, allowing for up to two 6K displays or one 8K display at 60Hz.

Notable updates include the **12MP Center Stage camera**, **nano-texture** display option, and **redesigned Thunderbolt 4 ports**. The colour options remain the same, though hues are lighter, and all colours are now available in both two-port and four-port models.

Summary of Key Features of iMac M4

1. **M4 Chip**: More efficient with higher performance.

2. **4.5K Retina Display**: True Tone technology and optional nano-texture glass

3. **Enhanced Graphics**: Better graphics support.

4. **Apple Intelligence**: AI-based productivity tools in macOS Sequoia.

5. **Improved Connectivity**: Wi-Fi 6E, Bluetooth 5.3, and added Thunderbolt 4/USB-C ports.

6. **Upgraded Camera and Audio**: 12MP camera with Desk View, studio-quality mics, and six-speaker system with Dolby Atmos.

7. **Colour Options and Accessories**: Seven colour choices with colour-matched accessories.

These updates make the 2024 iMac a robust choice for those who need powerful performance and elegant design.

System requirements and compatibility

The iMac with the M4 chip is designed with compatibility and performance in mind, aligning with modern hardware and software standards. It supports **macOS Sequoia** out of the box, optimized for the M4's advanced processing and AI capabilities. With the macOS system's updated multitasking features, new privacy controls, and integration with iPhone mirroring, you will enjoy a unified Apple ecosystem experience.

Hardware

Configured with options for up to **32GB unified memory** and storage choices of 512GB, 1TB, or 2TB SSDs, will allow you to handle intensive applications like media editing and software development. Its **Wi-Fi 6E**

and Bluetooth 5.3 ensure faster and more reliable wireless connectivity, while Thunderbolt 4 ports (4x) enable high-speed data transfer and multi-display support, suitable for professionals who need robust peripheral setups.

Environment

This iMac requires **100-240V AC power** and operates within temperatures of 50° to 95°F (10° to 35°C), with humidity ranging from 5% to 90% (non-condensing), allowing flexible use in various work environments. It is also tested for operating altitudes up to 16,400 feet, making it reliable even in high-altitude locations.

For professionals and creatives, this iMac offers a seamless experience across apps like Final Cut Pro and Adobe Creative Suite, backed by macOS's advanced features tailored to the M4 chip. Regular software updates will ensure that the system stays optimized and compatible with future app and macOS updates.

FREQUENTLY ASKED QUESTIONS

Common Questions about Setup and Usage

1. How do I transfer data from my old Mac to my new iMac?

You can use **Migration Assistant** to transfer your data. Connect both Macs to the same network, then open Migration Assistant on your new iMac (found in Applications > Utilities) and follow the prompts to transfer files, applications, and settings from your old Mac.

2. Can I use my iMac with multiple users?

Yes, you can create multiple user accounts on your iMac. Go to **System Settings > Users & Groups** to add new users, allowing each person to have their personalized desktop and settings.

3. How do I reset my iMac to factory settings?

To factory reset your iMac, restart it and hold **Command + R** to enter Recovery Mode. From there, you can use Disk Utility to erase your startup disk and reinstall macOS. Make sure to back up any important data first.

Tips for Improving the Battery Life of Accessories

1. **Turn Off Accessories When Not in Use**: If you're using a Magic Mouse or keyboard, turn them off when you're done to save battery life.

2. **Check Battery Status**: Regularly monitor the battery status of your Bluetooth devices. You can view this in the Bluetooth settings by clicking on the device in the list.

3. **Optimize Settings**: For devices with customizable settings, reduce features like backlighting on keyboards or disable gesture controls on mice when not needed.

4. **Keep Devices Updated**: Make sure your accessories have the latest firmware updates to improve efficiency and battery performance.

5. **Avoid Extreme Temperatures**: Keep your devices at room temperature, as extreme heat or cold can affect battery life negatively.

Solutions for Common App Issues

1. **App Crashing or Not Responding**:

   o Force quit the app by right-clicking the app in the Dock and selecting **Force Quit**. You can also use **Command + Option + Esc** to open the Force Quit Applications window.

2. **Application Not Opening**:

   o Ensure the app is compatible with your macOS version. Try updating the app or reinstalling it from the App Store or the developer's website.

3. **Slow Performance**:

   o If apps are running slowly, check for updates to both macOS and the applications. You can also free up system resources by closing unused apps and restarting your iMac.

4. **App Permissions Issues**:

   o Some apps require specific permissions to function correctly. Go to **System Settings** > **Privacy & Security** to adjust permissions for location, camera, microphone, etc.